# WELSH CHEESE BOOK

Recipes by Angela Gray

Photographs by Harry Williams

with an Introduction by Eurwen Richards

GOMER PRESS
in association with the WDA

First Impression – 2003

ISBN 1 84323 201 4

The publishers gratefully acknowledge the photographs
provided by Llanboidy Cheesemakers (p. 26); Pant Mawr
farm (Preseli, p. 10); South Caernarfon Creameries Ltd.
(p. 5 & p. 32); Snowdonia Cheese Company (p. 30); Aeron
Valley Cheese Ltd. (p. 18); Caws Cenarth (p. 14 & p. 44).

*photo opposite:*
  Abergavenny cheeses

Printed in Wales at
Gomer Press, Llandysul, Ceredigion

# Contents

# Introduction: The Tradition of Cheesemaking in Wales

Cheese has been made from the early years of civilisation. Wherever man wandered with his flocks or herds, the available milk was preserved in the form of a 'cheese'. Archaeologists working near Lake Constance on the Italian/Swiss border found a pottery colander, used to strain curds and whey, which dated back to the Stone Age. There are many references and no doubt legends showing that the people of ancient times used cheese both as an item of food and of commerce.

In Wales, records show that in 1552-53 quantities of both butter and cheese were shipped out of Glamorgan, and it can therefore be assumed that cheesemaking existed in the Principality long before then. During the seventeenth and eighteenth centuries there are many references to cheese being made and sold in the border counties of Clwyd and Brecon as well as in the Glamorgan area. Selling cheese to local shops and at fairs and markets was an important means of gaining a monetary return for any product that was surplus to family requirements.

In many areas it was customary to make cheese from skimmed milk, using the cream for the more profitable butter.

When the skimming was done by hand, there would have been sufficient fat left in the milk to make an 'edible' cheese. However, with the use of the more efficient mechanical separator, there are derogatory comments on the final quality, and mention is made regarding the 'toughness' of the cheese. Cow's milk (usually skimmed milk), was often mixed with sheep's milk, when that was available, and that made a richer, better quality cheese.

Although Caerphilly is known as the 'Welsh' cheese, many other varieties were made, and indeed the recipe for Caerphilly was not a standard one, even into the twentieth century. The storage conditions also influenced the end product. Caerphilly cheese was normally stored in a dry room, giving the final product its characteristic creamy white colour. However, there were farms where the storeroom was 'underground'. There, the conditions were suited to the growth of a blue mould and a natural blue Caerphilly cheese was the result.

That part of Wales that borders the Cheshire plain made a type of Cheshire cheese. This was sold locally, at the Chester fair and on to Liverpool. Cheese fairs were widespread – in Ruabon, Llanffestiniog, Haverfordwest, Brecon, Caerphilly, to name but a few. Some were weekly events, but others occurred annually.

Farmhouse cheesemaking continued into the early part of the twentieth century. Although there had been much standardisation by then, the quality and the type of the cheese continued to vary. There is reference in the reports of Bedwellty Show (1901) of 'Cwcw' cheese, i.e. the first cheese of the season, a softer more moist cheese than later in the year, and also of sage cheese. The addition of sage, as chopped leaves in the body of the cheese or as a decoration on the surface, added variety as well as providing valuable nutrients to the diet.

The nineteenth century was a period of change, with improved farming methods and increased mechanisation causing a greater awareness of the need to understand the process of cheesemaking and improving quality. During the last decade of the nineteenth century cheese grading began at the Caerphilly market.

The proliferation of local cheese-making classes and the development of dairy education at colleges in Aberystwyth, Glynllifon, Llysfasi, Usk, Pibwrlwyd and Gelli Aur was the result of a growing desire to improve academic knowledge as

*Cheesemaking at Llanboidy*

well as develop the craft of cheesemaking. Local classes continued well into the 1920s. In 1967 the Dairy Department at Aberystwyth was closed, later followed by the other colleges. These days formal dairy courses are held at Food Centres in Wales.

Industrialisation and the rapidly increasing populations in cities such as Cardiff, Liverpool and London made it easier and more profitable to send fresh milk to these areas than make cheese and butter on the farm. Milk collection depots were established in rural areas at the beginning of the twentieth century, many with a direct rail link to the big cities. In west Wales, creameries developed close to the railway at Capel Dewi, Llandysul, Pontllanio and Felinfach. These are but historical names now.

The milk depot at Four Crosses, Llanymynech started in 1902. It later became a cheese factory making Cheshire and the more traditional brined Caerphilly cheese. Cheese was regularly sent to Liverpool and Whitchurch in Shropshire. In 1957 the Milk Marketing Board purchased the factory. This cheese factory, like many other small units, gained high acclaim for the quality of its produce, but that did not prevent its closure in 1993.

A Farmers Co-operative began at Aberarad, Newcastle Emlyn in 1920 but ran into difficulties and was closed. It reopened in 1930 and in 1932 they began to make Caerphilly cheese there and then in 1936 they started making Cheddar. The cheese was sent by train to Highbridge in Somerset. The factory was closed in 1983 but was reopened in 1989, and today Mozzarella cheese is made there for the pizza market using the latest state-of-the-art technology.

In 1933 the Milk Marketing Board for England and Wales was formed. Farmers had a guaranteed market for their milk and found it much easier to send that milk to the factories than continue to make cheese on the farm. Farmhouse cheesemaking in effect ceased at that time. Caerphilly cheese was not allowed to be made during the 1939-45 war, but after those years, the factories diversified and made other varieties such as Double Gloucester, Leicester, and Derby with Cheddar. Later they were allowed to make Caerphilly cheese.

Many Welsh creameries were among the first to take advantage of advances in cheesemaking technology. The CWS factory at Corwen had the first BelSiro equipment from Australia. In 1971 Unigate installed the first of the new generation of mechanised cheesemaking units at Newcastle Emlyn. One tonne presses and boxes for maturing were installed at Johnstown. In 1977 a new creamery was opened at Maelor. This was closed as a cheesemaking unit in 1993, with the site being devoted to the pre-packing of cheese.

There have been many changes during the later half of the twentieth century with rationalisation of manufacturing as well as the installation of new technologies. Despite closures, cheesemaking and pre-packing continues in a number of creameries in north and west Wales.

The South Caernarfon Creamery at Rhydygwystl is the most long-standing of the Co-operative Societies in Wales. After a very shaky start in 1938, but with vision and entrepreneurial management, the factory has been to the fore in using modern technology and developing different varieties of cheese. They continue to win numerous awards for their cheese, together with acclaim for their achievements in the export market.

These days Caerphilly cheese is once again being made in Caerphilly. The quality of the cheese made at Castle Dairies is among the best, as has been recognised in the awards gained at various competitive events, including the British Cheese Awards.

In 1988 a new purpose-built creamery was opened in the Aeron Valley. This unit combines the latest technology of cheesemaking with the pre-packing of portions suited to the retail trade. The creamery is now owned by a collective of Welsh and Irish farmers, and continues to make a much sought-after product.

The introduction of milk quotas in 1984 no doubt contributed to a revival of interest in farmhouse cheesemaking. Many farmers suddenly found themselves in a position of possibly having to pay a levy on their now over-quota milk. Although some felt that the craft of traditional cheesemaking had been lost, there remained a remnant that could recall how the traditional cheese of Wales had been made and were pleased to assist in reviving those skills.

By today there are many farmhouse cheesemakers in Wales, who produce a wide variety of cheese from the milk of

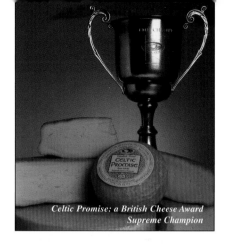

*Celtic Promise: a British Cheese Award Supreme Champion*

cows, sheep, goats and even buffalos. Caws Cenarth and Caws Nantybwla are two examples of traditional Caerphilly at its best. Llangloffan, Llanboidy, Gorwydd, Merlin, Cerwyn, Caerfai, Acorn, Lammas, Snowdonia, Abergavenny Fine Foods and Teifi are among the well known names, and not only within Wales. Each cheese has its own character and story, reflecting the passion of its makers, from the music of Leon Downey to the Dutch expertise of Patrice Savage-Onstwedder. Space will not permit the telling of these tales. What can be said is that each cheesemaker has given farmhouse cheese a new and exciting life.

The recipes, the method of manufacture will differ, and so will the milk. The delight of small scale

7

cheesemaking is, that in addition to the skill of the cheesemaker, the regional differences in the soil, the pastures, the type and breed of animal can be seen and tasted in the cheese. Some manufacturers continue to make cheese from raw milk. That is an added bonus, for the natural milk flora will add to the final flavour of the cheese.

Cheese with added flavours have increased in popularity. Many cheese-makers have extended their range of products by blending special mixes such as that for Y Fenni or including the flavour e.g. laverbread, garlic and herbs, with the cheese during its making

Whatever type of cheese is being made, there is always a need to ensure the safety of the product and each cheesemaker, large and small, is totally committed to this. The emphasis on hygiene and cleanliness is as relevant today as a century ago. The standards are rigorously applied, with modern technology to assist in the chemical and microbial testing providing the assurance of product safety as well as quality.

Farmhouse cheese has undergone a revival in Wales. The quality is second to none, as can be seen in the many Awards gained at the Nantwich International Cheese Show, the British Cheese Awards, the World Cheese Awards and other, possibly less prestigious shows, but still serious competition.

The Teifi Celtic Promise, a small washed rind cheese more typical of some European types than what has been considered a Welsh cheese, was Supreme Champion at the 1998 British Cheese Awards.

A new maker from Anglesey won much acclaim and a gold award for 'Gorau Glas' at the 2002 British Cheese Awards.

In spite of the increasing regulatory demands on our small-scale cheese-makers, they are continuing to make individual cheese of character. There is an exciting future, with more varieties being made for those customers who are discerning and seeking something different from the large-scale factory cheese.

Many cheesemakers consider raising awarness of their craft to be part of their mission, and for that reason, several farmhouse dairies welcome visitors – either regularly during Spring and Summer, or on special occasions. (Visitors would do well to plan excursions only after checking availability). There is little doubt that cheeselovers will take home their favourites and make good use of the mouthwatering recipes in this book.

EURWEN RICHARDS

# Starters

*Preseli from Pantmawr Farmhouse Cheeses*

# BAKED PRESELI CHEESE
### with roasted tomatoes and olives

Preseli cheese is perfect for this recipe. The soft rind helps to keep the cheese inside during the melt-down in cooking. You can serve it in its entirety, and use the toasted bread for dipping, or you can plate it up for a more lavish starter to your menu. It also makes a delicious lunch or supper dish. You may like to try this recipe with Perl Wen or Heritage cheese, which are great alternatives.

Preheat oven to gas 5, 190°C, 375°F. Place the slices of bread on a baking sheet and bake in the oven for about 20 minutes until lightly toasted. Remove from the oven and rub both sides with garlic. Put the whole Preseli cheese in a baking dish and top with the sliced garlic, sprigs of thyme or rosemary, then drizzle with a little olive oil. Bake in the oven for 20 minutes until soft and oozing. Make a simple dressing by mixing together the olive oil, wine vinegar, sugar, salt and pepper. Dress the mixed leaves. To serve, simply place the toasted bread on to serving plates, top with a wedge of the melting cheese and garnish with the dressed leaves, olives and roasted tomatoes.

Note: The baked tomatoes are delicious, so make them in bulk and store them in a sealed jar covered with oil. You can add flavour using herbs, chillies and garlic. To make the roasted tomatoes, cut them in half and place on a wire rack. Bake on the lowest oven temperature setting for at least 3 hours until they have reduced in size by half, cool and place in preserving jars.

### Ingredients serve 8

1 Preseli cheese or use the
    equivalent weight (250-350g/
    8-12oz) of any of the other
    suggested cheeses
4 sprigs of thyme or rosemary
2 cloves garlic sliced
Olive oil for drizzling

Garnish:
24 small roasted tomatoes
24 black olives
1 large clove garlic
4 tablespoons olive oil
2 tablespoons white wine vinegar
Salt and pepper
Pinch sugar
8 thick slices of French bread
Mixed leaves for garnishing

# Welsh Cheese Patties with a Salsa Dressing

This is a variation of the much loved Glamorgan sausage, using the influence of the Mediterranean to give a zesty alternative.

## Ingredients serve 8

175g/6oz white breadcrumbs
100g/4oz grated Organic Caerphilly
    cheese,
50g/2oz red onion, finely chopped
1 large garlic clove, finely chopped
50g/2oz red pepper, finely chopped,
1 tablespoon chopped basil
Salt and pepper
1 teaspoon Welsh mustard
2 egg yolks
Vegetable oil for frying

Salsa:
6 tomatoes, chopped
1 clove garlic, chopped
1 small red onion, peeled and
    chopped
2 tablespoons chopped coriander
4 tablespoons of lime or lemon juice
Salt and pepper
1 teaspoon chopped green chilli
Pinch sugar

Garnish:
Salad leaves
4 tablespoons salad dressing
Fresh coriander

First make the salsa by placing all the ingredients into a bowl and mixing well. Cover with clingfilm and refrigerate.

To make the patties, heat a little oil in a frying pan and cook the onion, pepper and garlic together until soft, remove from the heat and cool.

Mix the breadcrumbs and cheese together, then add the onion mixture, mustard, basil, seasoning and the egg yolks. Mix to form a dough, divide into 16 portions and shape into rounds.

Heat a little oil in a frying pan and cook the patties in batches over a medium heat until golden.

To serve, place the patties on a serving plate and garnish with some mixed, dressed salad leaves, coriander and a good spoon full of salsa.

Note: If you wish to make the traditional Glamorgan sausage, substitute the onion, pepper and garlic with 1 small, chopped leek, 1 tablespoon chopped onion and 1 tablespoon of chopped parsley, sauté until soft in some butter. Shape into sausage shapes and cook in the usual way.

# LAYERED WELSH CHEESE

Smoked Cenarth is ideal for making the cheese crisps for this recipe, whilst the filling uses a speciality cheese, Little Acorn's Noson Lawen, made with Worcestershire sauce and cashew nuts. However, you can choose from a wide range of cheeses such as Harlech or Tintern from Abergavenny Fine Foods, or one of the speciality cheeses from the Merlin range.

Oven temperature: Gas 6, 200°C 400°F

Brush two baking trays with a little vegetable oil. Divide the smoked Cenarth into 16 small mounds; flatten out slightly to form the size of a small biscuit. Place in a preheated oven and bake until golden. Remove from the oven, ease the cheese crisps off the baking sheet with a palate knife and leave to cool.

To make the filling place all the ingredients in a food processor, and whizz to form a smooth paste.

To assemble the dish place a small spoon of the creamed cheese mixture on to the centre of a serving plate, top at a slight angle with a cheese crisp. Repeat with more of the creamed cheese, finishing with a cheese crisp.

Mix together the cucumber, tomato or pepper and the capers, and spoon tiny mounds of the mixture around the outside of the layered cheese. Drizzle a little olive oil and lemon juice around and top with some chives or flat leaf parsley.

Note: The cheese crisps can be kept once cooled in an airtight container. They are great broken up in salads or as a canapé base. The creamed cheese makes a great cheese pate, which can also be used as a stuffing or in sauces.

### Ingredients serve 8

225g/8oz smoked Cenarth cheese, grated

Filling:
225g/8oz Little Acorn's Noson Lawen cheese, grated
225g/8oz cream cheese
1 clove garlic, peeled and grated
60ml/2floz white wine
1 tablespoon chopped chives

Garnish:
Rocket leaves
2 tablespoons finely chopped cucumber
2 tablespoons finely chopped red pepper or skinned tomato flesh
1 tablespoon of small capers
4 tablespoons olive oil
2 tablespoon fresh lemon juice

*Llangloffan farmhouse cheese*

# CONTINENTAL BREADS STUFFED WITH WELSH CHEESES

Oven temperatures: Gas 7, 220°C, 425°F then Gas 5, 190°C, 375°F

Dissolve the yeast in 4 tablespoons of the warm water, leave for about 20 minutes until it starts to ferment. Sift the flour together with the salt into a large mixing bowl, pour in the yeast, olive oil and the remaining water. Mix well to form a dough.

Turn the dough out on to a floured surface and knead for a few minutes until the dough is smooth. Place in a greased, clean bowl, cover with a clean tea towel and leave in a warm place until it is double in size.

Knock back the dough and divide into two, knead each portion until smooth. Flatten out one portion and place the sun-dried tomatoes, basil and cheese along the centre. Bring in both sides of the dough to the middle and seal in the filling. Place the bread on a greased baking tray fold side down, brush with egg wash and dust with a little flour. Bake in a preheated oven at the higher temperature for 15 minutes; reduce to the lower temperature and cook for a further 20-25 minutes. Remove and leave to cool on a wire rack.

Mould the second portion of dough into a 20cm (8-inch) round, place on a greased baking tray. Cut the cheese into large cubes and press them into the dough. Break off small sprigs of rosemary and press them halfway into the dough. Glaze with egg wash and sprinkle with sea salt, bake in the oven at the same temperatures and length of time as the first bread.

## Ingredients make 2 large loaves, or 16-18 rolls

15g/¹/₂oz compressed yeast or
1 tablespoon dry yeast
500ml/16floz lukewarm water
750g/1¹/₂lb bread flour (more if needed)
1 tablespoon salt
3 tablespoons olive oil
1 egg beaten and mixed with
¹/₂ teaspoon of salt for glazing

Bread filling 1:
6 sun-dried tomatoes
1 handful fresh basil
225g/8oz Caerphilly cheese e.g.
    Organic Caerphilly, Gorwydd,
    Cenarth, Nantybwla or Caerfai

Bread filling 2:
2 sprigs rosemary
1 teaspoon sea salt: Halen Môn
225g/8oz Welsh farmhouse cheese,
    e.g. Llanboidy, Llangloffan or
    Teifi

# Welsh Cheese and Laverbread Soufflés

You can use any cheese you like to make a soufflé; however, the fuller the flavour, the better the result. You can choose from a wide range of mature Welsh cheese such as: Llangadog, Llanboidy, Llangloffan, Snowdonia, Caws Celtica Beltane, Caws Llŷn mature and Welsh Gold.

Oven temperatures: Gas 4, 180°C, 350°F and Gas 6, 200°C, 400°F

Heat together the milk, cream, peppercorns, bay leaf, onion, garlic and nutmeg. Bring to near boiling point, remove from the heat, cover the pan and leave to cool. In a clean saucepan, melt the butter, stir in the flour and cook for one minute. Strain the milk into a jug and add to the flour a little at a time whisking all the time. Bring to the boil stirring constantly, reduce the heat and cook for 2 minutes.

Add the cheese and melt into the sauce. Stir in the mustard and season to taste. Allow the mixture to cool slightly then add the egg yolks and mix in well. Whisk the egg white to form soft peaks and fold gently into the sauce. Divide the mixture between the buttered ramekins, spoon in a little laverbread into the centre and place in a roasting tin with a little water. Bake in the oven at the first temperature for approximately 15 minutes until set, but not risen. Remove from the oven, allow to cool then refrigerate (you can make them to this stage and store in the refrigerator for 3 days, or freeze up to 1 month).

Grease a baking tray, using a small knife turn out the soufflés on to the sheet and bake in a preheated oven at the higher temperature for 20-25 minutes until puffed and golden.

## Ingredients serve 8

375ml/12floz milk
125ml/4floz double cream
1 bay leaf
4 peppercorns
1 slice onion
1 clove garlic
A little grated nutmeg
50g/2oz butter
50g/2oz flour
Salt and pepper
1 teaspoon Welsh mustard
225g/8oz mature Welsh cheese
100g/4oz laverbread
Butter for greasing ramekins

# Sticky Onion Tart with Teifi Cheese

Oven temperature: Gas 7, 220°C, 425°F

Grease a round 20cm (8-inch) cake tin with the butter.

Heat the sugar and butter together in a large frying pan over a medium heat, allow the sugar to dissolve and add the balsamic or sherry vinegar. Place the onions on top of the liquid together with the slices of garlic, season and increase the heat slightly.

## Ingredients serve 6-8

15g/½oz butter for greasing
150g/5oz caster sugar
300g/11oz red onions, peeled and cut into 2.5cm (1inch) slices
3 garlic cloves, peeled and sliced
50g/2oz butter
Salt and pepper
2 tablespoons balsamic or sherry vinegar
175g/6oz puff pastry
200g/8oz Teifi cheese, or Penbryn or St. Davids

Garnish:
Freshly ground black pepper and flat leaf parsley

Place a lid over the pan and allow the onions to cook through; the onions should be slightly caramelised on the bottom. Remove from the heat and allow to cool slightly.

Meanwhile roll out a pastry circle large enough to cover the cake tin.

Arrange the onions on the greased base of the cake tin and top with the pastry, tucking down the edge all the way around.

Bake in the oven for 25 minutes. Remove from the oven and turn out on to a baking tray, arrange the slices of cheese around, and place under a hot grill until golden. Sprinkle with freshly ground black pepper and garnish with flat leaf parsley.

# Main Courses

## Ingredients serve 8-10

Pastry:
175g/7oz plain flour
75g/3oz butter, cut into pieces
50g/2oz Nantybwla, Cenarth or
    Caerphilly cheese, grated
1 egg yolk
½ teaspoon salt
1 tablespoon of chopped chives or
    a teaspoon of thyme
1 teaspoon mustard powder
3 tablespoons water (more if
    needed)

Filling:
3 leeks, cleaned, trimmed, sliced
    and sautéed until soft
4 hard boiled eggs, shelled and
    sliced
225g/8oz Llangloffan farmhouse
    cheese or a similar mature
    Welsh cheese

Béchamel sauce:
600ml/1 pint milk
300ml/ ½pint double cream
1 bay leaf
slice of carrot
small stick celery
slice of onion
6 peppercorns
1 clove garlic
Salt to taste
50g/2oz butter
50g/2oz flour

# CREAMY LEEK TART MADE WITH TWO WELSH CHEESES

This recipe uses a cheese pastry which also makes wonderful cheese biscuits. Choose a more mature cheese such as Llangadog, Llanboidy, Llangloffan, Snowdonia, Welsh Gold, Caws Celtica Beltane or Caws Llŷn mature for the sauce.

Oven temperature: Gas 5, 190°C, 375°F

To make the pastry, sift the flour, mustard powder and salt into a mixing bowl. Rub the butter into the flour and make a well in the centre. Place the yolk, water, cheese and herbs in the well and gradually mix in with the flour and butter to form a dough. Roll out on a floured surface and line a 25cm, 10-inch buttered tart tin. Chill for 20 minutes. Line the pastry shell with baking parchment and baking beans, bake blind in a preheated oven for 25 minutes. Remove parchment and beans and cook for a further 15 minutes until the shell is golden and firm.

To make the sauce, heat together the milk, cream, bay leaf, peppercorns, carrot, celery, onion, garlic and nutmeg. Bring almost to the boil, remove from the heat and cover with a lid, leave to cool. Strain the flavoured milk into a jug. In a clean saucepan, melt the butter, stir in the flour and cook for one minute. Add the milk a little at a time to the flour, whisking all the time. Bring to the boil, stirring constantly, reduce the heat and cook for 2 minutes. Add the cheese and melt into the sauce.

Place the cooked leeks into the pastry shell, arrange the sliced egg on top, then pour over the cheese sauce. Top with the remaining grated cheese and the breadcrumbs, place under a hot grill until golden and serve.

# SPINACH AND MUSHROOM PANCAKES WITH Y FENNI CHEESE

With these pancakes anything goes: Y Fenni cheese is the perfect partner for the spinach and mushrooms, but you can use almost any Welsh cheese to give these pancakes real character.

## Ingredients serve 8

Batter:
100g/4oz plain flour
Pinch salt
250ml/8floz milk
3 eggs
25g/1oz butter
50g/2oz melted butter for frying
1 tablespoon chopped herbs

Filling:
450g/1lb mushrooms, sliced
450g/1lb spinach
50g/2oz butter
Salt and pepper
1 clove garlic, peeled and grated
Béchamel sauce-
750ml/1¼ pint milk
150ml/¼pint double cream
225g/8oz Y Fenni cheese
1 bay leaf, slice of carrot, small
    stick celery, slice of onion
6 peppercorns, 1 clove garlic,
    Salt to taste
50g/2oz butter
50g/2oz flour

Garnish:
50g/2oz Y Fenni cheese
50g/2oz white breadcrumbs

To make the pancakes, sift the flour into a bowl together with the salt. Make a well in the centre, break in the eggs and whisk until thoroughly mixed. Gradually pour in the milk making a smooth batter, then stir in the herbs. Heat a heavy-based pan or a crepe pan, add the 25g/1oz butter, cover the surface of the pan with the butter and pour the excess butter into the batter. Ladle enough of the batter into the heated pan to make a thin coating. When the edges start to curl up, use a palate knife to flip the pancake over. Cook until lightly browned, remove and place on a plate. Repeat until the all the batter is used up.

To make the sauce, heat together the milk, cream, bay leaf, peppercorns, carrot, celery, onion, garlic and nutmeg. Bring almost to the boil, remove from the heat and cover with a lid, leave to cool. Strain the flavoured milk into a jug. In a clean saucepan, melt the butter, stir in the flour and cook for one minute. Add the milk a little at a time, whisking all the time. Bring to the boil stirring constantly, reduce the heat and cook for 2 minutes. Add the cheese and melt into the sauce.

For the filling, melt the butter over a medium heat, add the garlic and cook for a minute, add the mushrooms and season. Cook over a medium to high heat for about 4 minutes. Pile in the spinach and cover with a lid; cook for a further 3 minutes until the spinach is wilted. Add to the cheese sauce. Divide the filling between the pancakes and roll up. Place in individual heatproof dishes or in a large dish, sprinkle with the remaining cheese and breadcrumbs and grill until golden.

Note: These can be made in advance and heated in the oven for 30 minutes at gas 5, 190°C, 375°F.

*Llanboidy cheese*

# LLANBOIDY VEGETABLE RAREBIT WITH LAVERBREAD

Any good flavoured cheese can be used to make a rarebit: this recipe uses a farmhouse cheese containing laverbread, making it quite a unique and exciting ingredient for this dish. Alternatively, use Y Fenni cheese, made with mustard seed and ale: this too has a great flavour.

Heat a griddle pan or a large heavy-based frying pan, brush the vegetables with olive oil, season with the spiced salt, or just sea salt and black pepper. Cook in batches until scorched and quite soft, keep warm.
To make the rarebit, heat the ale, add the cheese and melt slowly. Stir in the flour and cook for 2 minutes, add the mustard and mix well. Remove from the heat and mix in the egg.

Divide the vegetables into heatproof dishes, or make one large dish, top with the rarebit and bake in a pre-heated oven for approximately 15 minutes. Serve with a crisp salad and crusty bread.

Note: You can use any combination of vegetables such as spinach and mushroom, cauliflower, broccoli and spring onion, leek, potato and garlic or roasted mixed root vegetables. It's also luxurious on top of chicken breasts and Welsh fillet steak.

## Ingredients serve 6

Welsh rarebit:
225g/8oz Llanboidy with laverbread
or a mature Welsh cheese
4 tablespoons Welsh ale
1 teaspoon Welsh mustard
1 dessertspoon flour
1 egg

Vegetables:
2 red pepper, cut into 6 lengthways,
seeds removed
2 yellow pepper, cut into 6
lengthways, seeds removed
2 green pepper, cut into 6
lengthways, seeds removed
1 small aubergine, cut into 12 slices
2 red onions, peeled and sliced into
12 sections
6 cloves garlic, peeled and cut in half
2 courgettes, cut into 12 pieces
Olive oil for brushing
A little fresh oregano, basil or chives
for sprinkling
18 cherry tomatoes
Halen Môn spiced salt (optional) or
plain sea salt and black pepper

# Celtic Fondue

Fondues were extremely popular in the 60s and 70s and were great fun. Once you have your molten cheese, you can use all sorts of ingredients for dipping. Chargrilled vegetables are delicious, as are large garlic croutons and spicy cooked chunks of pork, chicken or beef.

Rub the inside of a fondue pot with the clove of garlic, pour in the wine and heat. Grate the cheeses and add to the fondue pot, cook to a creamy consistency. Mix the cornflour with the kirsch and pour into the melted cheese when bubbling. Season to taste and then place over an alcohol burner on a metal tray at the table. Serve with your choice of dipping ingredients.

### Ingredients serve 6

1 garlic clove, peeled
150ml/¼pint dry white wine e.g.
   'Cyfuniad' sych (Pant Teg) or
   'Cariad' dry
600g/1lb 4oz Celtic Promise or
   St Davids cheese
15g/½oz cornflour
50ml/2floz kirsch
Salt and pepper
A little grated nutmeg

# ROSTI WITH SKIRRID AND CARMARTHEN HAM

This recipe uses Little Acorn's Skirrid cheese which has been marinated in mead, giving it quite a delicate but distinct flavour. However you can also use cheeses such as St. Florence or Caws Celtica's Lammas. In fact just about any good melting cheese you like.

Cook the potatoes whole and unpeeled, for about 10 minutes in salted boiling water, drain and leave until cool enough to handle. Using a sharp knife remove the skins and grate the potatoes into a bowl, season well with salt and black pepper. Mix in the parsley, grated Skirrid and Chopped Carmarthen ham.

Melt half the butter together with half the olive oil in a 25cm (10 inch) heavy-based frying pan. Spoon the rosti mix into the pan pressing down to flatten it out. Cook for about 15 minutes over a medium to low heat.

Remove from the heat and turn the rosti out on to a baking sheet. Melt the remaining butter together with the olive oil, ease the rosti back into the pan, uncooked side down and cook for a further 15 minutes.

Serve either straight from the pan, or turn out on to a plate.

Ingredients serve 4-6

1.35kg/3lb even-sized Desiree potatoes
50g/2oz butter
1 tablespoon olive oil
Salt and freshly ground black pepper
75g/3oz Carmarthen ham, cut into small pieces
or cooked cured bacon
100g/4oz Skirrid cheese, grated
25g/1oz flat leaf parsley

# SNOWDONIA COBBLER

Oven temperatures: Gas 5, 180°C, 375°F then Gas 7, 220°C, 425°F

Heat half of the oil in a heavy-based pan. Mix together the flour, salt and pepper, coat the pieces of beef and fry in batches until golden brown. Remove and place in a casserole dish. Add the remaining oil to the pan and brown the vegetables together with the sugar. Place in the casserole dish. Add the stock to the pan to remove meat and vegetable residue, pour into the casserole. Add the wine and bay leaf. Cover and cook in a preheated oven for 1½ hours.

Meanwhile make the cobbler. Sieve the flour and salt into a mixing bowl, rub the butter into the flour and add the herbs and 150g/6oz of the grated cheese. Mix the egg, milk and horseradish together and fold into the flour mixture.

Mix together the butter and flour, add a little at a time to the casserole, stirring constantly. Divide the cobbler mixture into 8 portions and place on top of the casserole (leave the portions rustic, not formed), top with the remaining cheese and bake in the oven at the higher temperature for 20 minutes until the top is golden brown.

## Ingredients serve 8

900g/2lb Welsh stewing beef, trimmed
2 tablespoons of flour
1 teaspoon salt
1 teaspoon black pepper
1 bay leaf
2 large onions, peeled and chopped
2 large carrots, peeled and chopped
1 large stick celery, chopped
1 small parsnip, peeled and chopped
1 clove garlic, peeled and chopped
6 table-spoons oil
1 teaspoon sugar
600ml/1pint beef stock
6ooml/1 pint red wine

To thicken:
25g/1oz butter
25g/1oz flour

| Cobbler: | |
|---|---|
| 200g/8oz flour | 1 teaspoon horseradish |
| 25g/1oz butter | 1 tablespoon chopped parsley |
| 200g/8oz Snowdonia cheese | 2 eggs |
| | 2 tablespoons milk |

30

# Raised Pork Pie with Mature Welsh Cheddar

Oven temperatures: Gas 6, 200°C, 400°F and Gas 3, 160°C, 325°F

Melt the butter in a pan, add the leek, celery and onion, cook for 2 minutes then add the garlic, apricots and apple and cook for a further 2 minutes. Pour in the cider and add the lemon rind, sage, seasoning and mace, mix well and simmer for 10 minutes, leave to cool. In a large mixing bowl, mix together the sausage meat, cooked ingredients, cheese and breadcrumbs.

Divide the pastry into 3 portions. Grease and flour a 20cm (8-inch) loose bottom cake tin, roll out one portion of the pastry to line the base, another to make the sides, secure the side to the base with a little beaten egg. Fill the tin with the pork and cheese mixture, roll out the third portion of pastry for the top, secure with a little beaten egg. Use any trimmings of pastry to make a design on the top. Glaze with beaten egg, place at the centre of the oven and cook in a preheated oven at the first temperature for 30 minutes. Reduce the temperature and cook for a further 40 minutes. Remove and allow to cool, ease the pie out of the loose bottom cake tin, and ease off the base with a palate knife. Serve with a crisp salad and pickles.

## Ingredients serve 8-10

350g/12oz good quality sausage meat
25g/1oz butter
3 sticks celery, chopped
1 small leek, cleaned and chopped
12 'ready to eat' apricots
2 eating apples, peeled, cored and chopped
150g/6oz mature Welsh Cheddar e.g. Llangadog,
Caws Llŷn or Welsh Gold cheese
1 onion, peeled and chopped
2 cloves garlic, peeled and chopped
2 tablespoons chopped, fresh sage
100g/4oz fresh breadcrumbs
50g/2oz pistachio nuts (optional)
Grated rind of a lemon
125ml/4floz Welsh cider
$\frac{1}{2}$ teaspoon ground mace
600g/1$\frac{1}{2}$lbs shortcrust pastry
Salt and pepper
1 egg, beaten for glazing

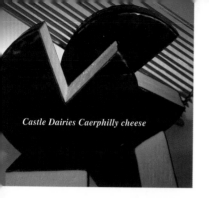

*Castle Dairies Caerphilly cheese*

## SPINACH AND CAERPHILLY CHEESE FILO PIE

Oven temperatures: Gas 3, 170°C, 325°F and Gas 7, 220°C, 425°F

Place the chopped spinach and spring onion in a large bowl, mix with a tablespoon of salt and leave for 30 minutes. Put the mixture in a clean tea towel and squeeze out the liquid. Place mixture in a bowl and combine with the nutmeg, eggs, cheese, dill and black pepper.

Melt the butter, line the base of an ovenproof dish measuring 30 x 20cm (12 x 8 inches) with a sheet of filo. Brush with melted butter, and repeat until the base is 4 sheets thick. Top with the spinach and cheese mixture, then make a top with the remaining 4 sheets of filo pastry, buttering in between and brushing the top with butter.

Bake in a pre-heated oven for 45 minutes, then increase the heat and cook for a further 5 minutes until the top is golden. Serve warm with a tomato salad.

### Ingredients serve 6

1kg/2lb 4oz fresh spinach, washed and finely chopped
225g/8oz spring onions, trimmed and finely chopped
300g/10oz Caerphilly cheese, crumbled
2 eggs
$\frac{1}{2}$ teaspoon grated nutmeg
175g/6oz butter
1 tablespoon chopped fresh dill
1 x 400g pack filo pastry
Salt and pepper

# HADDOCK AND PRAWN SMOKIE

## Ingredients serve 6

450g/1lb puff pastry
100g/4oz mature Welsh cheddar
100g/4oz smoked Welsh cheese
  e.g. Cenarth, Celtica,
  Nantybwla, South Caernarfon,
  Teifi, Corwen or Minola
  Caerphilly
500g/1lb2oz smoked haddock,
  filleted and skinned
100g/4oz peeled prawns (raw tiger
  prawns if possible)
50g/2oz smoked 'back' bacon
3 spring onions, chopped
12 button mushrooms
Freshly ground black pepper
750ml/1½pints béchamel sauce
  (see page 22)
1 beaten egg
2 tablespoons fresh chopped
  parsley

Oven Temperature: Gas 6, 200°C, 400°F

Roll out the puff pastry and make 6 vol-au-vent cases: you need 6 x 10cm (4-inch) round or square bases, cut another 6 rounds the same size, cut a smaller round or square out of them to form the edges and lids. Assemble the vol-au-vents on a damp baking tray attaching the edges to the base with a little of the beaten egg, mark the lids with a design. Brush the surface of the edges and the lids with beaten egg, place in the pre-heated oven and bake for 20-25 minutes until well risen and golden. Meanwhile make the béchamel sauce, add the two cheeses and allow to melt. Cook the pieces of bacon in a little butter; when lightly browned add the mushrooms and cook for 2 minutes. Cut the haddock into chunks and add to the hot sauce, After 2 minutes add the prawns, bacon and mushrooms. Season with freshly ground black pepper and stir in the chopped parsley.

Remove the vol-au-vent cases from the oven and place on serving plates. Divide the filling between the cases and top with the pastry lids.
Serve with new potatoes and green beans.

# BLOODY GRANSTON

Granston Blue is a full flavoured farmhouse cheese from Llangloffan, which is perfect for this recipe. Also suitable are Perl Las, a delicious creamy cheese, and Gorau Glas from Anglesey, a really classy 'blue'.

Oven temperature: Gas 5, 190°C, 375°F

To make the sauce, heat the olive oil in a pan, add the onions and celery cook until softened. Add the garlic and bay leaf, cook for a further 2 minutes allowing the vegetables to brown lightly. Pour in the white wine and tomatoes, bring to the boil and reduce to a simmer. Add the Tobasco, Worcestershire sauce, sugar and seasoning, check taste. Cook the sauce slowly for about 40 minutes until quite concentrated. Pour in the Vodka and add the oregano, cook for a further 10 minutes. If the sauce become too dry just add a little more white wine. Whilst the sauce is cooking, prepare and cook the chicken. Cut a deep pocket into the side of each chicken breast and season. Cut the cheese into 6 slices and stuff each slice into the pockets. Season the flour with the salt, lightly dust each breast with the flour, shaking off the excess. Dip each one into the beaten egg, then into the breadcrumbs (If using pine nuts, roughly chop them and add to the breadcrumbs). Melt the butter in a heavy base frying pan, seal the breaded chicken on both sides for about 2 minutes over a medium heat until lightly golden. Remove the chicken from the pan into an oven dish. Bake in a pre-heated oven for 25-30 minutes.

To serve, ladle some of the sauce onto serving plates and place a chicken breast in the centre. For pure indulgence, serve with garlic mash and steamed asparagus.

## Ingredients serve 6

6 chicken breasts, skinned
350g/12oz Granston Blue cheese
50g/2oz butter
Salt and black pepper
1 tablespoon flour
$\frac{1}{2}$ teaspoon salt
175g/6oz breadcrumbs
1 tablespoon pine nuts (optional)
1 egg beaten

Sauce:
1 onion, peeled and finely chopped
2 cloves garlic, peeled and finely chopped
1 stick celery, chopped
2 tablespoons light olive oil
450g/1lb tinned plum tomatoes
150ml/5floz white wine
1 dessert spoon of Worcestershire sauce
1 dessert spoon of Tobasco sauce
1 teaspoon sugar
Salt and pepper
150ml/5floz Vodka
1 tablespoon chopped fresh oregano

*Penbryn farmhouse cheese*

# WELSH PORK PENBRYN

There is excellent quality pork being produced in Wales these days. In this recipe escalopes of pork are wrapped up with an irresistible mix of fragrant basil, juicy pine nuts and the very tasty Penbryn cheese. Alternatively you could use other cheeses such as Teifi or St.Florence.

Put all the ingredients for the filling into a food processor and blitz for a few seconds to form a coarse mixture. Divide the filling between the pork escalopes, place in the centre, tuck the edges in and roll up, secure with a cocktail stick.

Mix the salt with the flour and lightly dust the pork rolls. Melt the butter in a heavy-based pan and seal the meat on all sides, reduce the heat and cover with a lid, cook for approximately 10 minutes, turning occasionally.

When cooked through, remove from the pan and keep warm.

Increase the heat, pour in the wines and the lemon juice, bring to the boil then reduce the heat and simmer for 5 minutes. Mix together the butter and flour and whisk into the sauce, continuing to whisk until the sauce has thickened slightly. If the sauce reduces too much just add a little water to bring back the consistency. This is wonderful served with a mushroom risotto. However, potato dauphines and steamed seasonal vegetables also make for a fabulous accompaniment.

### Ingredients serve 6

6 x 175g/6oz Welsh pork
    escalopes, flattened out
Salt and pepper

Filling:
75g/3oz pine nuts
A handful of fresh basil
175g/6oz Penbryn cheese
1 clove garlic
Zest of 1 lemon
1 tablespoon flour
$1/2$ teaspoon salt
50g/2oz butter

Sauce:
150ml/$1/4$ pint Marsala wine
200ml/7floz red wine
Juice of a lemon
15g/$1/2$oz butter
15g/$1/2$oz flour

# WELSH SEAFOOD GRATIN

Oven temperature- Gas 5,190°C, 375°F

Cook the pasta in a large saucepan of salted boiling water. Drain well.

Make the béchamel sauce, add the cheese, mustard, grated garlic and cayenne pepper. Divide the pasta between 6 gratin dishes, or use one large oven dish.

Top with the seafood and season lightly. Pour over the sauce and top with the breadcrumbs. Cook for 25-30 minutes in a pre-heated oven.

Garnish with the slices of lime and sprigs of flat leaf parsley. Serve with new potatoes roasted with spiced Halen Môn salt and steamed seasonal greens.

### Ingredients serve 6

500g/1lb2oz large pasta shells or
    similar large pasta
175g/6oz cooked, large, peeled
    prawns
175g/6oz cooked crab
175g/6oz cooked cockles

Sauce:
750ml/1⅓ pints béchamel sauce
    (page 22)
225g/8oz Llangloffan red cheese
    with garlic and chives, or
    similar with garlic and chives
    from Merlin, Little Acorn,
    Teifi or Penbryn
1 teaspoon Welsh mustard
1 clove garlic
A flattened ¼ teaspoon cayenne
    pepper

Garnish:
6 slices lime or lemon
Flat leaf parsley and breadcrumbs

Desserts

*Caerfai 'Caerphilly' cheese*

# RHUBARB, STRAWBERRY AND CAERPHILLY CRUMBLE

Oven temperature: Gas 5, 190°C, 375°F

Top and tail the rhubarb and remove the stringy skin. Cut into 2.5cm (1-inch) lengths, place into a large heatproof dish, sprinkle with the sugar and the stem ginger with its syrup. Cut the strawberries in half and place on top.

Make the crumble by sifting the flour into a mixing bowl, then rub the butter into the flour until it resembles fine breadcrumbs. Crumble in the Caerphilly cheese, and stir in the sugar and orange zest. Spoon over the fruit and even out the surface.

Bake in a preheated oven for 30 minutes; remove, then drizzle the top with the honey. Return to the oven and bake for a further 10 minutes. Serve warm with some whipped cream, organic Greek-style yoghurt or some Welsh vanilla ice cream.

## Ingredients serve 6

750g/1lb 10oz rhubarb
300g/10oz strawberries
100g/4oz sugar
2 tablespoons stem ginger
   (preserved) chopped

Crumble:
225g/8oz plain flour
100g/4oz butter
75g/3oz Caerphilly cheese
Zest of ½ an orange
75g/3oz Demerara sugar
1 tablespoon Welsh honey

42

# DEEP FRIED PERL WEN WITH PLUMS IN ELDERBERRY PORT

This is so good! The plums can be made in advance and kept in the refrigerator for up to 4 days. If plums are not in season then use summer fruits, but just warm them through in the port syrup. Caramelised apples and oranges are also excellent with this indulgent dessert.

To make the plums in port, heat together the port, orange juice, bay leaf and sugar. Stir until the sugar is dissolved, bring to the boil, reduce the heat and simmer for 5 minutes. Add the redcurrant jelly and stir until dissolved. Add the plums and poach until just cooked through. Keep warm, or cool and refrigerate if making in advance.

To make the batter, mix together the flour and sugar, make a well and add the egg yolks and milk, mix to a smooth batter. Whisk the egg white and fold into the batter.

Heat the cooking oil to 190°C (375°F). Remove the rind from the Perl Wen and cut into 18 cubes. Dip the cubes of cheese in the batter and fry in batches in the hot oil until golden, turning occasionally. Remove and drain on kitchen paper. Plate with a serving of the plums in elderberry port, dust the deep-fried cheese with icing sugar.

## Ingredients serve 8

Batter:
175g/6oz plain flour
2 eggs, separated
50g/2oz caster sugar
125ml/4floz milk
Oil for deep-frying
Icing sugar for dusting

Plums in elderberry port:
450g/1lb red plums, halved and
    stoned
200ml/7floz Cwm Deri elderberry
    port
Juice of 1 orange
100g/4oz caster sugar
4 tablespoons redcurrant jelly
1 bay leaf

Cheese:
1 Perl Wen 300g/11oz round
    miniature

*Pantysgawn cheeses*

# Pantysgawn Cheesecake with Summer Fruits and Black Mountain Liqueur

### Ingredients serve 8

250g/9oz Jordan's cereal with
   strawberries or raspberries or
   use digestive biscuits or a good
   museli as a base
75g/3oz melted butter
1 tablespoon Welsh runny honey

Filling:
450g/1lb plain Pantysgawn goats'
   cheese
300ml/½ pint double cream
Juice of 1 lemon
2 tablespoon welsh runny honey
3 drops vanilla essence

Topping:
700g/1lb9oz mixed fresh summer
   berries: strawberries,
   raspberries, blackcurrants,
   redcurrants, blueberries,
   loganberries etc
150ml/¼pt Black Mountain liqueur
75g/3oz caster sugar
Mint leaves for garnishing

Pantysgawn goats' cheese is so mild in flavour you can use it in both savoury and sweet dishes. It's wonderful marinated in olive oil with herbs, garlic and chillies. This recipe uses its versatility with fruit, which is a superb match. You can make 8 individual cheesecakes using 'chef' rings, or make one large one in a 20cm (8-inch) loose bottom cake tin.

To make the base, place the cereal or biscuits into a food processor together with the honey and melted butter. Whizz until the ingredients break down and start to stick together. Spoon into the base of a loose bottom tin, or into the bottom of 'chef' moulds on dessert plates. Press the base in firmly and chill in the refrigerator.

Meanwhile make the filling, Mash the cheese together with the lemon juice, honey and vanilla until smooth. Whip the double cream into soft peaks and fold into the cheese. Spoon on top of the base and even out, place back in the refrigerater to chill for at least 3 hours: overnight is good.

To make the topping, heat together the liqueur and sugar until dissolved. Add 225g/8oz of the berries to the liqueur and cook for 5 minutes. Pass through a sieve to remove the seeds and retain the sauce.

To finish, run a knife around the inside edge of the cake tin to release the cheesecake. Push the base up through the cake ring and place the cheesecake on a serving plate. Arrange the fruit on the top and drizzle the fruit and liqueur sauce over the top. Finish with sprigs of mint and serve.

# Marinated Apricots Filled with Welsh Cheese

This dish is stunning as part of a buffet; the fruits can also be served as sweet canapés.

To make the syrup, heat together the liqueur, apple juice, whole spices and sugar. Stir until the sugar is dissolved, bring to the boil, reduce the heat to a slow boil and cook until the liquid resembles a thick syrup.

Cut a pocket into each of the apricots, divide the cheese into 24 portions, roll into balls and fill the pockets. Arrange on a serving plate, pour the syrup over the top, and finish with chopped pistachio nuts.

These are delicious served in the warm syrup with some Welsh vanilla ice cream.

Note: The syrup can be made well in advance, and the entire dish can be assembled and refrigerated for up to 3 days. Serve at room temperature.

### Ingredients serve 8

24 'ready to eat' dried apricots
350g/12oz Pantysgawn goats' cheese.

Syrup:
150ml/¼ pint 'Danzy Jones' whisky liqueur
150ml/¼ pint apple juice
1 cinnamon stick
1 star anise
4 green cardamom pods
2 cloves
175g/6oz caster sugar
100g/4oz pistachio nuts to finish

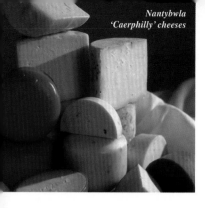

# AFTERNOON FRUIT AND CHEESE CAKE

Oven temperature: Gas 4, 175°C, 350°F

Grease a 23-25cm (9-10-inch) cake tin and line the base with baking parchment. Cream together the butter and sugar until light and creamy. Beat the eggs in one at a time. Sift the flour and baking powder together into a bowl and add to the butter mix a little at a time. Add the mixed spice, apricots, nuts, apple, sultanas and cheese, and fold in. Spoon into the prepared tin, smooth out the surface and sprinkle with the Demerara.

Bake the cake in a preheated oven for 45-55 minutes. Remove from the oven and leave to cool slightly, then ease out of the cake tin and cool on a wire rack.

Note: This cake is also delicious served warm with custard.

### Ingredients serve 8-10 portions

250g/8oz flour
1 tablespoon baking powder
Pinch salt
250g/8oz Welsh butter
250g/8oz dark brown sugar
4 eggs
1 teaspoon vanilla essence
1 dessertspoon mixed spice
Grated zest of a lemon
100g/4oz dried apricots, chopped
75g/3oz sultanas
50g/2oz chopped hazelnuts
2 apples, peeled quartered, cored
    and grated
125g/5oz Caerphilly cheese
1 tablespoon Demerara sugar

# Gooseberry and Llanboidy Puffs

Oven temperature: Gas 6, 200°C, 400°F

Roll out the pastry and cut out 8 x 12.5cm (5-inch) squares. Brush the edges with a little beaten egg, fold in slightly to form a thin collar all the way around. Pinch the corners and twist. Place on a damp baking tray and top with the gooseberries. Mix together the sugar, zest, juice, ginger and cheese.

Divide the mixture into 8 portions and spoon on top of the gooseberries. Brush the edges with beaten egg, and bake in a preheated oven for approximately 20-25 minutes until risen and golden on top. Remove from the oven, dust with icing sugar and serve with whipped cream mixed with a little elderflower cordial.

### Ingredients make 8

900g/2lb puff pastry
450g/1lb gooseberries topped and
    tailed
75g/3oz soft brown sugar
25g/1oz stem ginger, chopped
Zest of ½ orange
2 tablespoons orange juice
100g/4oz Llanboidy or another
    Welsh farmhouse cheese
Icing sugar for dusting
1 beaten egg for glazing

# Sauces
# and Dips

# Welsh Cheese Pesto

Although Pesto is traditionally made with Parmesan cheese, some of the Welsh mature cheeses are ideal – the more mature the farmhouse cheese, the dryer and more concentrated the flavour. Look out for locally grown basil in the summer months, for it has so much more flavour than the forced grown.

If you are making this in a food processor, puree the basil together with the garlic, pine nuts, cheeses and 3 tablespoons of the olive oil. Then pour in the remaining olive oil and season to taste with salt and pepper.

If you are using a mortar and pestle, chop the basil and add to the mortar with the garlic, pine nuts and cheese. Mix and pound the ingredients until thoroughly combined, forming a smooth paste. Gradually add the olive oil, season with salt and pepper.

Note: You can substitute the basil with flat leaf parsley, chervil, mint or coriander. You can also add another flavour dimension by adding 1 tablespoon of sun-dried tomatoes or roasted red pepper. To give it a real Welsh flavour make it with 1 tablespoon of laverbread and 1 tablespoon fresh chopped parsley instead of the basil.

Use as a sauce for pasta, mix in with mashed potato, in rice and polenta, or simply drizzle over salad potatoes. It's wonderful as a topping for fish or chicken and also with roasted lamb and Mediterranean style roasted vegetables. It's also great as part of a stuffing, for example in bread and for finishing off soups such as minestrone.

### Ingredients make 450ml/¾pint

50g/2oz basil leaves
100g/4oz mature Welsh farmhouse
    cheese e.g. Llanboidy or
    Llangloffan
50g/2oz pine nuts
Salt and pepper
175ml/6floz olive oil

# Easy Pasta Sauce with Leeks and Welsh Cheese

Heat the olive oil in a large pan, add the leeks and cook over a low heat until soft, but still vibrant in colour. Add the garlic and cook for 2 minutes. Remove from the heat and place the leek mixture in a blender together with the herbs, wine, cheese and egg yolks. Process to form a thick, smooth sauce; season to taste.

### Ingredients make 600ml/1 pint

1 large leek, washed trimmed and chopped
2 cloves garlic, peeled and chopped
Salt and pepper
1 tablespoon chopped parsley
1 tablespoon basil
300ml/½ pint white wine e.g. 'Sugar loaf' medium or 'Glyndŵr' medium
50ml/2floz olive oil
125g/5oz of Caerphilly type e.g. Nantybwla, Caerfai, Cenarth, Gorwydd, or Organic Caerphilly
2 egg yolks

Note: this sauce can also be made with 175g/6oz roasted Mediterranean vegetables, or the same quantity of roasted onions and garlic mixed.

Use the sauce over cooked pasta – simply drain the pasta, return to the hot pan, place over a low heat, pour in the sauce and mix well. Garnish with fresh basil and oven roasted tomatoes.

This sauce is also wonderful with cooked potatoes and vegetables. Place the cooked vegetables or potatoes in an oven dish, cover with the sauce, sprinkle with a little more grated cheese and breadcrumbs and bake in a moderate oven for 25 minutes.

# Welsh Cheese, Herb and Garlic Dip

Place all the ingredients in a food processor and blend to form a smooth dip. Decant into a bowl, cover and refrigerate for up to 3 days. Serve at room temperature.

Note: If you wanted a stronger flavour you can mix in 50g/2oz of Granston Blue or a speciality cheese such as Llandyrnog Red Leicester with chillies.

Ingredients make 300ml/½pint

100g/4oz soft goats' cheese e.g. Pantysgawn or Pant Mawr
100g/4oz organic Greek-style yoghurt
50ml/2floz milk
50ml/2floz white wine
1 tablespoon mixed fresh herbs e.g. chives, chervil, basil, coriander, parsley
1 clove garlic peeled and finely chopped
1 tablespoon finely chopped red onion
¼ teaspoon medium hot chilli (optional)
Salt and pepper

Serve with fresh vegetables for dipping, or as a dressing for potato salad. Spoon into hot jacket potatoes, or on top of barbecued burgers, and vegetable burgers. Pan-fry a load of mushrooms in a little butter and serve with a spoon of this dip and large croutons.

# Y Fenni Cheese Dip

Place all the ingredients into a food processor and whizz to form a thick paste. Decant into a bowl, cover and refrigerate up to 5 days.

Note: This dip is the ultimate indulgence for your oven-roasted fat chips. Cut up 4 large potatoes into fat wedges, and 2 red onions. Place in a roasting tray and drizzle with a little vegetable oil, shaking the pan so that they are coated with the oil. Sprinkle over a tablespoon of Halen Môn salt with spices. Roast in a hot oven for approximately 40 minutes until golden and crisp.

This dip is also great for filling jacket potatoes, or potato skins. Melt under the grill on toast or over sliced tomatoes. Spoon over a Welsh fillet of beef and finish off in the oven, or spread over some oven-baked pork sausages and allow to melt in the oven.

Ingredients make 300ml/½ pint

125g/5oz Y Fenni cheese
75g/3oz cream cheese
1 teaspoon mustard
2 spring onions, finely chopped
100ml/4floz Welsh ale
Salt and pepper

# WELSH CHEESE PATE

Place all the ingredients in a food processor and whizz to form a thick paste. Spoon into a bowl or if you want to turn it out, into a mould lined with clingfilm, and refrigerate. Serve with fresh crusty bread and pickles.

### Ingredients serve 6

225g/8oz Mature Welsh cheese
  e.g. Granston Blue, Organic
  Llanboidy, Snowdonia, Caws
  Llŷn, Llangadog, Welsh Gold
100g/4oz cream cheese
50g/2oz soft butter
50ml/2floz port

Note: The pate can be divided into ramekins and topped with either chopped herbs, melted butter and sliced gherkin or chopped nuts and celery; serve with hot toast and a salad garnish. For a starter the pate can be stuffed into ripe pear halves, and served with a watercress and walnut salad. Serve it on croutons to accompany an onion soup, or use as a topping for meat and vegetable dishes.

# SMOKEY CHEESE SALAD DRESSING

Place the cheeses and cream/milk into a food processor and mix to a thin paste. Add the onion and herbs and whizz for a few seconds. Chop the bacon into small pieces, pour the dressing into a bowl, add the bacon and season to taste.

Note: Serve with any salad – it's particularly tasty with crisp green lettuce and large croutons.

### Ingredients make 300ml/¹/₂pint

25g/1oz finely chopped red onion
50g/2oz cooked smokey bacon
1 tablespoon chives
75g/3oz cream cheese
50g/2oz smoked Welsh cheese
    e.g. Cenarth, Caws Celtica,
    Nantybwla, South Caernarfon
    and Teifi
100ml/4floz single cream or milk
Salt and pepper

## FURTHER INFORMATION:

- A number of the cheesemakers in Wales formed a cooperative in 2003 in order to ensure that their produce is widely available both within Wales and further afield. If readers have enquiries – about the cheeses, the cheesemakers, the shops where the cheeses may be bought or the restaurants where Welsh cheeseboards are in evidence – then please contact David Evans, chair of Cheeses from Wales Ltd. at cheesesfromwales.co.uk

- Some cheesemakers have the space and facilities for visitors and indicate on their brochures when cheesemaking might be observed. Please note that not all cheesemakers are set up for this. If you are interested in paying a visit, do check first.

- A number of farmhouse cheese producers have their own websites. Try keying in the name of the cheese and you could well track down the site.

- For more information about Welsh food, go to the WDA's comprehensive websites:

www.walesthetruetaste.com
www.cymruygwirflas.com

The second website noted is in Welsh.
*Mae'r ail wefan yn un Gymraeg.*

Alternatively, the telephone information line is 08457 775 577